GO HERE, see ELSEWHERE

poems by

Prairie Markussen

Finishing Line Press
Georgetown, Kentucky

GO HERE, see ELSEWHERE

Copyright © 2021 by Prairie Markussen
ISBN 978-1-64662-477-5 First Edition
All rights reserved under International and Pan-American Copyright Conventions. No part of this book may be reproduced in any manner whatsoever without written permission from the publisher, except in the case of brief quotations embodied in critical articles and reviews.

ACKNOWLEDGMENTS

This chapbook has been a long time coming. I want to thank my husband, Joe, for encouraging me to keep working at these poems over the years, between jobs and baby and PhD program. Thank you, Joe, for always reminding me that these poems should make a move from my computer into the world.

I also want to thank Nick Smith, fellow poet and excellent critic, for giving me feedback on this manuscript many moons ago. These poems are in better shape now because of his wisdom and insight.

And thank you to my many poetry teachers, who, in different ways, challenged me to dig deeper, go further, and write what I love.

Publisher: Leah Huete de Maines
Editor: Christen Kincaid
Cover Art: Joseph Sass
Author Photo: Joseph Sass
Cover Design: Elizabeth Maines McCleavy

Printed in the USA on acid-free paper.
Order online: www.finishinglinepress.com
also available on amazon.com

Author inquiries and mail orders:
Finishing Line Press
P. O. Box 1626
Georgetown, Kentucky 40324
U. S. A.

Table of Contents

IN THE DICTIONARY OF IMAGINARY PLACES 1
ABATON 2
BABAR'S KINGDOM, see CELESTEVILLE 3
CABBALUSSA 4
DADDY JONES' KINGDOM 5
EAR ISLANDS 6
FAIRYLAND 7
GAALDINE, see GONDAD 8
HACIOCRAM or ISLE OF PROPHETS 9
IANICUM, see LAMIAN 10
JABBEROO, see LOONARIE 11
K, VALLEY OF, see ALIFBAY 12
LACELAND 13
MABARON or DOUBT 14
In the NAVEL OF LIMBO 15
OBALSA, see WISDOM, ISLES OF 16
PA-ANCH 17
QUEEN ISLAND, or THE DOG'S PERSPECTIVE 18
RAKLMANI: I Imagine Maria 19
SABA 21
TACARIGUA 22
UDOLPHO 23
VAGON 24
WAFERDANOS 25
X 26
YAMS, ISLE OF or TEENAGE YAMIAN ANGST 27
ZAK, see SOUTHERN SEA 28

For Joe, my unfailing cheerleader
For Ceridwen, my goddess of poetry

Author's Note

These poems were inspired by *The Dictionary of Imaginary Places*, edited by Alberto Manguel and Gianni Guadalupi. *The Dictionary of Imaginary Places* is a wonderful compendium of imaginary places found in literature from the 2nd century AD up to present time.

IN THE DICTIONARY OF IMAGINARY PLACES

For Tom Nolan

I found
your funeral program
and your face staring up from the glossy
white paper
I had been looking for the Glittering Caves (see Aglarond)
for Neverwhere, for the Joyous Isle
found instead years (1957-2011)
found instead a name, real,
not imaginary
the list of songs we sung, the first
and second readings
and finally, the fireman's prayer
I must have put the program there
no other book large enough or sturdy
enough to press the paper
smooth
I never found *The Song of the Crew*
though the index pointed me toward it

I leave you, smiling, between the lime green
end sheets, while the rest of us
float   between
the Saharan Sea and the Blazing World,
searching for your song.

ABATON

> *"(from the Greek a, not; baino, I go), a town of changing location. Though not inaccessible, no one has ever reached it . . ."*

No one ever believed she was from Abaton,
born and bred within the mysterious interior
of its walls. Who could verify?

Old Tom at the bakery says he once saw
white towers rising above a thick mist,
and a fiery glow. Ms. Finch
from the school crosses her heart and hopes
to die that she had heard a harpsichord
playing the most mournful tune. Niall,
the smithy, waves it all away with a blackened
hand, and maintains the city walls were
the palest blue, nearing white. But Old Tom
is a drunk, and Ms. Finch an old maid,
and Niall's blue-eyed bride left him years ago.

There is no one. And she, when questioned,
when interrogated, won't say for certain.
Won't confess the color of the walls, won't
tell the height of the magnificent towers, will not
even say who plays the harpsichord, though Niall
swears her fingertips are calloused.

She will only say Abaton is her home,
and is lost beyond its gates. Ms. Finch
and Old Tom exchange a look: they never saw
gates.

She wanders between Glasgow and Troon,
a litany of colors falling from her lips, rejoicing and weeping
in equal measure at the improbable horizon.

BABAR'S KINGDOM, see CELESTEVILLE

The real problem was never between
King Babar and King Rataxes, tyrannical
though he might have been in Rhino Land.

The real problem was between the king himself
and his queen consort, Celeste. On a whim,
while still in the full flush of first love, Babar

decided to name the capitol of his kingdom after his own
beloved bride, and not, as Cornelius (Secretary
of Defense and Minister of Foreign Affairs)

had hoped, after Babar himself. Cornelius felt
it gave the Queen too much clout. Pompadour and Troubadour
agreed. And though the land was still

officially Babar's Kingdom by name, it more often
than not was known as Celesteville. Cornelius thought
this name lacked gravitas, was less than impressive, and belied

a certain weakness. But none of this ever bothered
King Babar until he discovered his beloved queen
knocking tusks with Truffles, the palace cook.

It was only then that Babar realized how much power
he had let trickle from his trunk to hers. And so promptly
he bedded Ursula, Celeste's best friend. Not moments after

he called an urgent meeting with Cornelius, Pompadour,
and Troubadour. Celesteville no more. Babar's Kingdom
from here on out. The three agreed and struck

Celeste and her name from history.

CABBALUSSA

Anthropophagous (adj): cannibalistic; inclined to eat human flesh.

somewhere in the Atlantic
lays an island
inhabited by Indian women
fierce and hooved
dangerous
who bed you
and wine you
and finally, eat you

why waste the wine?

(you'd think
after battling both
the King of the Moon
and the King of the Sun
over colonization of the Morning Star
you'd be able to withstand women
with ass hooves and dripping incisors)

why bother with cowards?

DADDY JONES' KINGDOM

      Oh Daddy,
how I loved Edward's brother.
You never knew his name,
but I did. That was a secret
between us. Like I
was your secret, Daddy.
Like I was a hushing sound between
your lips. I never wondered
why you did it—autocracies
are like that. What does not fit
is removed.
      Like me. Like Edward's
brother. I don't know about Edward,
but his brother never once tread
on a stranger, never once paid
for a funeral. And what they say
about his size is only half true.
He was tall, but not so tall
that he overshadowed me, not so tall
that I could not climb a ladder
to his lips.
      And the island you banished
us to? What better place—shaped
like a small heart and just as forgiving.

EAR ISLANDS

I wonder how the fish feel
when the fishermen come to hunt

with their burly bodies covered in ears
that twitch at every watery rustle.

None of the expected hiding places will do,
for even if a fish stays still

in some dark, rocky overhang, its tail
might twitch to keep it in place.

Or worse: the sound of the swim bladder
taking in or releasing oxygen,

forcing the fish to rise or to fall. It is
a spongy, low sound and is like gold to the fishermen.

      Only the eels are safe, as they burrow
deep into the mud. The fishermen hear

their movements, but cannot see them clearly.
The fish tell me it is better to be an eel.

FAIRYLAND

On the tenth day, I entered
the House of the Ogre, which lies
along the banks of an unnamed river.
I was tired. I had nearly been delivered
to the ash tree on the fourth day, and still
could not get over the shock.

I was cold. I couldn't remember
where my coat had gone. Perhaps
the beech tree, with its woman's voice
and its woman's form had taken it
as I stood swooning dumbly at its base.

I opened a closet door and then another,
searching the hut for something to cover myself—
and as I opened the fifth door, my shadow
came out to meet me. It walked with me
from room to room and shook as I shook
and brushed at its dusky limbs as I brushed
at mine. The shadow could not be given
the slip.

It went with me to the palace,
up and down the corridors, shooting
out from me in jagged angles.
It went with me to the library where I read
and read, hoping that in just one story
I'd be the hero, the adventurer, and not
the befuddled traveler who can't remember
why he came here in the first place, or why
his shadow continues to bother.

GAALDINE, see GONDAD

1.   If you look it's actually "Gondal"
not "GONDAD". It seems to me
this could have easily been cross-
checked. Merely follow your own
advice: GAALDINE, see GONDAD.

2.   Seems somewhat fitting, I suppose,
in a book of imaginary places.
To be pointed toward something
that not only never truly existed
beyond the poems of the Brontës,
but doesn't even exist here.

3.   Does that mean it does exist?
Double negatives canceling themselves
out to create a positive?

4.   Did Emily, Charlotte, and Branwell
go for GAALDINE, and see GONDAD
instead?

HACIOCRAM or ISLE OF PROPHETS

My house is like Haciocram:
    we all have our beliefs.
Except I'm not sure where the soul is; certainly
    not in the thumb or the big toe—those
dolty body parts.
If I could guess, I'd say the soul
    likes it cold and skims
right along the sclera. That's my coldest
    part. My brother would say different.
He'd say: who cares. Isn't that depressing?
    But that's how it is here. I could
convert him to my way of thinking—that
    is an option. Conversion by way of
torture. I've done it before.
    Didn't turn out though. He was only pretending.
He was crafty. And that is also an option here.
    You see what I mean, then: we are all prophets.
And rivals. Guards are up.

IANICUM, see LAMIAN

When there are worms in my tongue,
I make you taste them.
That's love. My suffering / your suffering.
Don't you find it strange
that the Italians want them
for poison? The worms, I mean.
Not our suffering. No one
wants that. Do you ever wonder
how the worms got there?
Growing in the hot bed
of my tongue? Only tempered
by flint. And then not even forever.

How many times
have you set herbs to the wounds?
How many times quieted
the roots of the problem?

JABBEROO, see LOONARIE

My mother could live on Jabberoo.
I'd put her there rather than Awdyoo,
the "Isle of Journalism, avoided by everyone."
I'd want her to have some friends.
On Jabberoo at least, there would be others
for her to talk at.

*

Nothing gets done, you see, because
they're always talking. Their desire
is insatiable. But not one of them
is saying a damn thing. It's just noise.
Jabber, if you'll allow me that laziness.

*

Strange, since my mother is fond
of cleanliness. Overly fond. And order.
Would she take talking over order?

*

Perhaps she belongs instead on Wotnekst.
There, the inhabitants have voted: their language
is the universal language. Doubtful
that Awdyoo or Jabberoo have gotten on board,
but Wotnekstians don't care about the other
Loonarie Islands.

*

Problem is, Wotnekst is also filthy.

K, VALLEY OF, see ALIFBAY

You wanted to go Here, see Elsewhere.
Greener, see Fence.

You wanted a Career, see Job.
Job, see None.

You wanted Arrow, see Boomerang.
Closure, see Memory.

You wanted Meaning, see Tone.
Tone, see Context.

You wanted Beginning, see K, Valley of.
K, Valley of, see Alifbay.

You wanted Alifbay, see Ending.
Ending,
       see Escape.

LACELAND

> *"As the traveler approaches the island, a region of bright light will suddenly appear against the shadows."*

The number of shadows is uncountable.
The traveler is used to the shadows.
The traveler travels by boat, and rows
at an even pace.
The shadows are the darkest of colors,
of purple potatoes and beets.

The island nears and its sudden bright light is fierce.
The traveler cannot see,
and places hand in front of eyes.
Fingers play and weave the light.
The island comes and goes across the eye
as geometric patterns, as blips and flits.

The traveler calls the island Laceland:
for all that is seen, there is still much
in shadow.

MABARON or DOUBT

From Lomb, go ten days
in any direction, and you'll reach Mabaron.

And once in Mabaron, find the city of Calamy,
where the Apostle rests—Saint Thomas.

His hand, his arm, are preserved,
and wait to settle disputes, to name victor or loser.

> *Thomas did not believe his man was dead, insisted
> he touch the wound.*
>
> *He was rebuked later, for not believing,
> for daring to look for the nails' dark drill.*

He waits, to decide, to make things plain;
with one flick of his dead hand, he casts aside doubt

so you don't have to.

In the NAVEL OF LIMBO

        the brain is made up of packages: four.
They are stacked and tied
with string, addressed, and ready for more
than merely to sit, off-kilter,
in the curve of the skull, covered in postage,
awaiting delivery. The problem
with the packages is not the problem
of escaping the cavity, or circumnavigating
all that bone—it's that their addresses are unknown.
Hastily or drunkenly or tiredly written,
the letters are misshapen like the country's counties.
Even to the Navel of Limbo, the postman
himself, the words are unguessable, ignorable. Strange, to call him
"postman."
He so rarely delivers a thing. He asks instead
the same question—too foolish to write or repeat—and moves
to the next house to ask it again.

OBALSA, see WISDOM, ISLES OF

"Neighboring Obalsa, by contrast, is ruled by the philosophy of 'as if.'"

I listened to the message again and again
    as if you'd never said it.
I believed in the bed we bought
    as if a third had never been there.
I loved the low-slung night best when I guzzled wine
    as if you didn't hear me.
I wrote a poem, two, three, four
    as if you enjoyed being my muse.
I met you at the park
    as if a talk would fix.
I went to the church and pressed beads into my palms
    as if I was heard.
I walked to the snowy drive, shovel in hand, and dug in
    as if I could dig myself out.

PA-ANCH

The myth: Many cities have risen here—
this island south of the Red Sea.

The fauna: elephants, lions, leopards.
The power: the priests',
they pick virgins, and
the land is held in common.

Strange: the artisans stand level
with the priests, but see no virgins.

The work: we till, and bring forth sugarcane,

And more: We mine:
gold, mostly, and other minerals.

The export: Myrrh, sent out
and burned at the feet of foreign soldiers.

The second myth: that we have never burned
it here. That there is no rebellion.

QUEEN ISLAND, or THE DOG'S PERSPECTIVE

It was the strangest thing:
one moment, he was hoisting
our flag at the peak, proud,
a fine black tea running
through his veins—the next
he was raving about bangers,
mash, and his mother's mutton.
He was bonkers.
        Back home, they say
he said nothing ever again.
He would only walk
toward the North Pole, again
and again, with a volcanic fire
burning like fever in his eyes.

As for me, I joined up with
another crew, and followed
doggedly, followed faithfully,
as I'd done with Hatteras,
as I'd always done,
right up to the brink and beyond.

RAKLMANI: I imagine Maria

Maria
        Maria, you were spare.
Your face: narrow, like a fence post.
Your hair slid upward into a child's knot.
Unremarkable; ugly, even.

*

Food
        You never ate, unless
it was ritual. Unless
it was for more than mere blood
sugar, than energy.
Energy can be found in many places:
the flick of eyes across Revelations;
the dry-fingering of beads;
the morning muttering.
Cheese and mutton: the least of these things.

*

Turin
        Did you want to be as slim
as His face on the shroud?
That dusty piece of linen.
I wonder: how many times
you visited that wall, to watch
Him hanging.

*

Desire
        That was the beauty—to have one
simple and sacred meal once a year.
To need not a scrap more.

*

Abnegation
        A yogi
told me: to breathe once an hour
would be the highest achievement.

*

Loss
        And what of the tastes?
What of the scents?

*

Life and Art
        In *Leggende del mare*, you wrote:
the Raklmani—saintly, pious—eat
only a blessed shell of an Easter egg,
once a year. They wait for the shell
to float to them. They wait for that sign
from lands across the immense sea.

*

Crux
        Just the shell. No yolk, no
albumin.

*

Purpose
        I imagine it crunching between her teeth,
white against white. Flecking her
with what cannot be digested
until she is as hard and faceless
as stone.

SABA

> "The people of Saba are born yellow and turn black as they grow older... Many of them suffer from dysentery and die young... Because of the heat, the rivers and waters of Saba are salty and the people lie in the water from dawn to noon to avoid the rays of the sun."

She was golden—my first love.
She shone from beneath the cool water
at the river. She was easy to find.
Oh, how often I lay down with her:
slipping slowly into the wet, letting it cover
my lackluster yellow.

Gripping the mossy stones at my left
and right, I would turn to her and speak
into the current. She would laugh
and toss her head, her hair a live and tendril thing.
Dew jewels at her tear ducts. We promised
never to turn black—never to suffer.
Salted and safe, we would rise to the surface,
and take in the dying light of day,
the apple trees, dropping their burdens
by the hour, and check every inch
of each other for that terrible shade.

TACARIGUA

I wore my tartan the day
I stepped off the ship and onto
the island.
        I came with ballet already
choreographed. Half a life spent
in the Edinburgh house between *Onegin*
and *Faust*.
I was free. The island air took me
by force—I awoke.
        I was a widow. Half a life
spent in black. But here, I wore
my clan—kelly green, canary yellow.
        I tell you—I was changed.
Spent too much time hiding beneath
my skirts; not enough twitching my hips
to a rhythm I thought had run its course.
        It woke. And flowed to the island's
Opera House. The ladies there, those lusty
Cunans. I taught them a thing or two, and more.
        No more Marguerite. Tatyana
from here on out. Tatyana from the hills
of Tacarigua to the highlands.

UDOLPHO

Udolpho (castle, two towers, a Marquis who offended)
before Udun (Mordor, the Mountains of Shadow)
before Uffa (an island, adventures, all untold)
before Ulmia (island alone)
before Ulthar (village near the Skai River, in Dreamworld)
before Ultima Thule, see Thule
before Under River (home to outcasts, fugitives, thieves)
before Universal Tap Room (walls of rock, taps to turn the weather)
before Unknown Island (jasmine across the Indian Ocean, the dog *barbu*)
before Unreturnable-Heaven (the road empty, the travel never recommended).

VAGON

I snuck in on the night they met,
the night before the quest that was not yet great
but would become so.

I made my way from Camelot—
it's not far—to Vagon, a castle cursed
with an ugly name, but pretty if compared to nothing.

All 150 of them, clanking
against the stone walls, and itching
to be gone. Forgotten their women

already. I wasn't special
to any one of them; I loved them all.
I hid behind tapestry after tapestry

as I snuck around the great room
to look one last time at each of them.
They didn't see me, but I looked,

and bid each one to come home.
In the end, only three returned.
I married one. And kept my eyes

on him alone.

WAFERDANOS

> "The wisest man amongst the Waferdanians is called "King of the People." Every morning he holds court on top of a high bamboo terrace called "The Temple." The entire population comes to greet him and to ask his advice. As soon as the session is over, the king becomes a commoner again just like the others, and joins the daily hunt."

I would never come down.
Bollocks to the daily hunt,
and to the noonday meal,
the love making and the game playing.

I have never been fond of nature.
My father, once King of the People,
told me I would grow out of this.
But he came down, too, like the others.
    So what does he know?

It's no wonder we're all bored
as often as not. Justice and brotherhood
and philosophy—they'd bore anyone eventually.
Someone has to be king.

I'd stay up. I'd grip the bamboo
and make them tear me town. When
those two ships came, those visitors,
I would have speared them through,

and not given them clothes to wear
from our precious *daquir*, not kept
them comfortable as they ascended
to the Temple and understood what
    we did not.

X

". . . no one knows why since no one plans to live there."

I built this place
but you are not planning to stay.

Pity: all the architecture,
all the intra- that went into.

I built according to your plans:
tight at the corners, claustrophobic

for safe-keeping. Some parts
expanding, others contracting.

It will never come down.
It will litter the shore

along with the others,
built to scale, built to suit,

and out of sync with all that came before.

YAMS, ISLE OF or TEENAGE YAMIAN ANGST

No, thank you.
Don't even talk to me about the nose salute,
or the *Pupera*, that lame
practice of presenting oneself
to the heir of our island, balancing
on our noses, upside down. So lame.

Don't talk to me about our local currency, either.
I'm sick of human teeth. Who cares?
Also, lowering my head
between my legs just because the king walks
by is totally fascist. And plus, I hate it.
I don't want to talk about any of it.
Seriously, by this tooth!

ZAK, see SOUTHERN SEA

Any number of places we could have met:
the spires of Thalarion,
the gardens of Zura,
the headlands which guard the harbor of Sona-Nyl.
Imagine:
the ivory spires, carved with lovers' tales;
the twist and turn of vines, leaves so lush they nearly burst with moisture;
the crystal headlands, those glistening sights.
Any of these.
Yet, we chose Zak. The terraces.
Beautiful in their way. But rife with temples,
the gods—old and new—so present,
so heavy. We could hardly breathe
for all the prayers. Better
that we had chosen the black towers
of Dylath-Leen. Better to have been honest
about what fates we were bringing down
on our own heads: flaunting our lust—
a woman, and another woman's husband.

Better to have gone past the architecture,
and straight to the sunken city in the sea.

Prairie Markussen lives and writes in Chicago currently, though she's lived and written in many places, including Los Angeles, Tucson, England, Wales, and South Korea. She recently received her PhD from the University of Arizona in Rhetoric, Composition, and the Teaching of English. She teaches writing for a community college in the Chicago area. Her work can be found in *Atticus Review, Painted Bride Quarterly, The Fiddlehead, Louisiana Literature.*

www.ingramcontent.com/pod-product-compliance
Lightning Source LLC
LaVergne TN
LVHW041506070426
835507LV00012B/1371